THE GOTHIC POETS DEPARTMENT

SONGS AND POEMS

RACHEL LAWSON

Contents

THE SEA OF TIME

I am lost in the sea of time,

I am merely a memory of seas gone by,

I am lost in time's wake,

Long forgotten is my world and time,

I am just a shadow of a shell, my old home,

Cry not for my loss, I am beauty in death's ardent clutch,

Death has no worry for the dead,

My world is dead, and my time is too,

I with the fishes of my seas swam in my era now I am just a neat relic

of past life on ancient Earth,

My bones have melted away and become part of my stone shadow, a

fossil

TEARS OF A CLOWN

I am Pierrot, don't call me a clown,

I bear the rose of a broken heart,

I lost my love to my rival,

So I cry, No, I do not lie,

Or will I lay down my rose, my heart.

My tears are my heart's lost blood,

I will die of grief before I lay down my rose,

My heart will die.

I am Pierrot, don't call me a clown,

I bear the rose of a broken heart,

I lost my love to my rival,

So I cry, No, I do not lie,

Or will I lay down my rose, my heart.

My tears are my heart's lost blood,

I will die of grief before I lay down my rose,

My heart will die.

DICK TURPIN & THE KING OF THE ROAD

Upon the road, Tom, the King of the road, met Turpin,

Dick thought Tom King was a fat pigeon,

they rode together on their way,

they robbed people with their guns under the code of the men of the highway,

"Your money or your life?" they did call,

it was nothing or all,

Tom made Turpin a highwayman legend,

it was rumoured Turpin brought King to his end,

Tom was shot in the shoulder,

he was taken to the Doctor,

he could not be saved,

Turpin, goodbye to the road he waved,

a butcher he became,

he was caught under a charge of a poaching claim,

he wrote a letter for help from one of his in-laws,

the only problem was the letter his death did cause,

an old teacher of Turpin's read through his fraud,

they knew his handwriting he told the truth and no one could save
him not even the good Lord.

he was revealed and caught,

the gallows called according to the court.

death came swiftly,

the legend grew greater hereby quickly.

Nevermore-Song

Nevermore shall I see your face in this world,

I am lost and alone,

I miss your smile,

You are lost to the world,

Sleeping in the eternal sleep of death,

In your cold grave,

I kneel by your grave,

I feel nearer to you,

Even though we are far from each other,

Between us are life and death,

The furthest distance in space and time,

I reach in my dreams to see you,

To hear your voice again,

I reach out to you in my dreams,

Only to have you disappear like a wisp,

In the wind,

You disappear,

To return to me Nevermore, Nevermore.

ECHOES OF MEMORY

Spoken

Don't worry, about the lost they are not really gone

as long as you can remember them

they still live.

Chorus

Nothing is truly lost,

Nothing is truly gone,

All things lost still remain,

They still stay alive in memory,

of those who were there.

Verse

In the march of time,

People and things are lost,

Things always change,

For better or worse,

Chorus

Nothing is truly lost,

Nothing is truly gone,

All things lost still remain,

They still stay alive in memory,

of those who were there.

Verse

Dreams come and go,

People are taken by the gathering storm of time,

Eras change in the ebb and wane of time,

They are lost in the sands of time,

Chorus

Nothing is truly lost,

Nothing is truly gone,

All things lost still remain,

They still stay alive in memory,

of those who were there.

Coda

Nothing is truly lost,

Nothing is truly gone,

All things lost still remain,

They still stay alive in memory,

of those who were there.

Spoken

Everything remains in memory

The Ravens

A flock of ravens floats upon the air over their prey,

Like a looming black storm cloud of gloom,

In the later hours of the death of the day,

They fight each other for room,

In the melee, one is injured it falls,

Blood and gore fill the air,

The air is filled with their dire calls,

Little did the observers of this carnage care,

To them, it was merely a display of the nature of the raven,

Upon the hour they fled,

They were neither crazed nor craven,

They were happy and well-fed.

ALL WE SEE OR SEEM IS BUT A DREAM WITHIN A DREAM BOOK

THEME SONG V2

Spoken plaintively

All we see or seem is but a dream within a dream

Chorus

My life is a series of secret lives,

I am more than what I seem,

no one sees who I truly am,

all they see is a dream of me,

All they see, or I seem, is but a dream within a dream

Verse

I am a mystery to the world,

I hide myself from the world,

I am just a dream to the world,

Chorus

My life is a series of secret lives,

I am more than what I seem,

no one sees who I truly am,

all they see is a dream of me,

All they see, or I seem, is but a dream within a dream,

Verse

They see me as many different men,

It is not fair they don't see me.

The truth they can't see,

Chorus

My life is a series of secret lives,

I am more than what I seem,

no one sees who I truly am,

all they see is a dream of me,

All they see, or I seem, is but a dream within a dream,

Coda

Like everyone else, all I see or seem is but a dream within a dream

All we see or seem is but a dream within a dream

WHERE DO DREAMS GO WHEN THEY DIE? - A SONG

Spoken

Where do dreams go when they die?

Chorus

Where do dreams go when they die?

Where do dreams go when you lose them?

What happens when a memory dies?

Verse

They are lost and forgotten, but why?

They are lost to time,

They are merely forgotten memories.

Chorus

Where do dreams go when they die?

Where do dreams go when you lose them?

What happens when a memory dies?

Verse

Why do we lose our dreams?

Why do we forget them?

Where do dreams go?

Chorus

Where do dreams go when they die?

Where do dreams go when you lose them?

What happens when a memory dies?

Coda

Where do dreams go when they die?

Where do dreams go when they die?

Where do dreams go when they die?

Spoken

Why do dreams have to die?

A GHOST OF A CHANCE

Death has come to me,

I am still alive, but I know death has come for me.

I haven't a ghost of a chance to live,

I have only one last prayer to give,

On my life's blood, I wish to live on,

My life is almost gone,

I haven't a ghost of a chance to live,

I have only one last prayer to give,

I have one last breath to take

From this sleep, I won't awake.

Death has come to me,

I am still alive, but I know death has come for me.

I haven't a ghost of a chance to live,

I have only one last prayer to give,

On my life's blood, I wish to live on,

My life is almost gone,

I haven't a ghost of a chance to live,

I have only one last prayer to give,

I have one last breath to take

From this sleep, I won't awake.

THE MAGICIANS SONG

You don't know the secrets beyond my smile,

I have a heart of darkness, I hide in plain sight,

You can't know my secret life beyond the light of day.

In the shadows of the night of my life,

I dwell in the shadows

Shadows of the Forgotten Realm - Song Theme for Vivienne and the Reaper

Death has become real to me,

I am lost in the realm of darkness,

I am going to a place where the living all dread,

I am going to the realm of the dead,

I am becoming merely one of the

Shadows of the Forgotten Realm

I am in the Shadow lands of the dead,

I am lost in the realm of the dead,

fear and horror are my nearest and dearest friends here in the Shadows of the Forgotten Realm.

Down here in the realm of the dead,

I fear where I'm going, I fear who I meet, I fear for my lost life in the Shadows of the Forgotten Realm

BEHIND HIS BLUE EYE - THEME TO THE MAGICIANS: BEHIND BLUE EYES

"Any ideas who John Doe is?"

"No,"

Chorus

No one knows the secrets he's hiding behind his blue eyes,

no one knows what he hides behind his blue eyes

Verse

He is the grim reaper in disguise

Chorus

No one knows the secrets he's hiding behind his blue eyes,

no one knows what he hides behind his blue eyes

Death does not come to him as a surprise,

He knows it is only a reprise,

Chorus

No one knows the secrets he's hiding behind his blue eyes,

no one knows what he hides behind his blue eyes

Death does not come to him as a surprise,

To the unknown dead he is wise,

Who they are he seldom does advise,

Chorus

No one knows the secrets he's hiding behind his blue eyes,

no one knows what he hides behind his blue eyes

From his death he does arise,

death his body does not compromise,

Chorus

He is the grim reaper in disguise

No one knows the secrets he's hiding behind his blue eyes,

no one knows what he hides behind his blue eyes

Death does not come to him as a surprise,

He knows it is only a reprise,

He is the grim reaper in disguise

Chorus

No one knows the secrets he's hiding behind his blue eyes,

no one knows what he hides behind his blue eyes

No one knows the secrets he's hiding behind his blue eyes,

no one knows what he hides behind his blue eyes,

behind his blue eyes,

behind his blue eyes,

behind his blue eyes,

The Magicians: The Ghost of Your Gaze or The Ghost's Serenade

Spoken

"What are you doing?"

"Why are you dressed as the Ghost?"

Chorus

I'm a ghost,

I'm not ghosting you.

I am here, although you don't see me,

I am here, but you can't hear me,

All you see is another man,

With my face, and form,

Verse 1

You can see me through his facade,

I am the one how truly loves you,

but you see me as only a friend,

to you, I am merely a shade of myself.

Chorus

I'm a ghost,

I'm not ghosting you.

I am here, although you don't see me,

I am here, but you can't hear me,

All you see is another man,

With my face, and form,

Chorus

I'm a ghost,

I'm not ghosting you.

I am here, although you don't see me,

I am here, but you can't hear me,

All you see is another man,

With my face, and form,

Verse 2

Why can't you see me beyond the echos of the past,

Why are you blind to my love?

Will you ever see me?

The true me

Chorus

I'm a ghost,

I'm not ghosting you.

I am here, although you don't see me,

I am here, but you can't hear me,

All you see is another man,

With my face, and form,

Coda

I'm a ghost,

I'm not ghosting you.

I am here, although you don't see me,

I am here, but you can't hear me,

All you see is another man,

With my face, and form,

Spoken

"But you are no Ghost he is charming and amazing, you are just...

You."

"Well, I could be him, he is very

mysterious,"

Masters of the Earth - The People From The Center of the Earth song theme

We are the star men

Chorus

We are the Star men,

masters of the Earth,

You can't take our place,

Verse

we run your world,

surface dwellers,

we own the earth

Chorus

We are the Star men,

masters of the Earth,

You can't take our place,

Verse

you can't take our place,

we live in your hollow planet,

we run your world without us

this planet will die.

Chorus

We are the Star men,

masters of the Earth,

You can't take our place,

Verse

we run your world,

surface dwellers,

we own the earth

Chorus

We are the Star men,

masters of the Earth,

You can't take our place.

Death Has Come For Me

Death has come for me,

No one can cheat death,

not even death himself,

death has come for me,

No one can cheat death,

not even death himself,

There is no way back from

death once he has come for you.

SEND IN THE CLOWNS BOOK THEME SONG

Send in the clowns,

The happy, friendly clowns,

Send in the clowns.

Masters of mirth and laughter,

Send in the clowns.

The happy, jolly clowns,

Send in the Clowns

We don't have any?

Send in the Clowns

These monsters anyway

THE MAGICIANS: DISILLUSIONMENT - SONG

Spoken

Why can't you see me?

I am not a dream,

I am not a fantasy

Look I am really here

Chorus

Why can't you see me beyond your dream of me,

I am not just a dream within your dream,

I am not a dream, I am me,

Verse

I am lost in your dreams,

You see me as a dream,

You know me am not a dream,

I am real.

Chorus

Why can't you see me beyond your dream of me,

I am not just a dream within your dream,

I am not a dream, I am me,

Verse

You know me,

I know you,

but why can't you see me

Chorus

Why can't you see me beyond your dream of me,

I am not just a dream within your dream,

I am not a dream, I am me,

Coda

Am not a dream

Spoken

Why can't you see me?

A DARKER SHADE OF SELF - A SONG

Spoken

Know this that even saints have a shadow side to their hearts

it is but a darker shade of self

Chorus

Even saints have a shadow side to their hearts

it is but a darker shade of self,

Verse

This side may be hidden deep within their soul

deep down,

It is their other half, may be not always their better part,

Chorus

Even saints have a shadow side to their hearts

it is but a darker shade of self,

Verse

They may not even be aware of this darker shade

within their soul hidden deep within

Chorus

Even saints have a shadow side to their hearts

it is but a darker shade of self,

Chorus

Even saints have a shadow side to their hearts

it is but a darker shade of self,

Coda

Even saints have a shadow side

Even saints have a shadow side

it is but a darker shade of self,

it is but a darker shade of self

TAKE ME AS I AM

Spoken passionate

I love you more than life,

and death won't end it, my love for you.

You gotta take me as I am,

I can't give you more than this,

I am just a poor man, nothing more can I give you,

All I have to give you is my love and my name,

I am not wealthy, but in love I am rich,

If I have your love,

I am the richest man in the world, with your love.

I can soar above the world,

With the hope you give me,

With your love and faith

I can do anything,

I could do anything you ask of me,

If you call me,

I would fly to your side,

You make me feel like I'm a superman,
your love makes me feel I can do anything,
The world and death can't stop my love for you,

You are an angel living in my heart,
I pray to you, that we will never part,
Spoken passionate
I love you!

AM I JUST A SHADOW YOU DREW? -SONG

Am I just a shadow you drew?
Am I just a ghost you never knew?
Am I only a dream in your mind?
Why were you so unkind?
If I am only a nightmare of your sleepless night,
I am lost in your world of terror and fright.
Am I just a shadow you drew?

Am I just a shadow you drew?
Am I just a ghost you never knew?
Am I only a dream in your mind?
Why were you so unkind?
If I am only a nightmare of your sleepless night,
I am lost in your world of terror and fright.
Am I just a shadow you drew?

Am I just a shadow you drew?
Am I just a ghost you never knew?
Am I only a dream in your mind?
Why were you so unkind?
If I am only a nightmare of your sleepless night,
I am lost in your world of terror and fright.
Am I just a shadow you drew?

Am I just a shadow you drew?
Am I just a ghost you never knew?
Am I only a dream in your mind?
Why were you so unkind?
If I am only a nightmare of your sleepless night,
I am lost in your world of terror and fright.
Am I just a shadow you drew?
Am I just a shadow you drew?

Am I just a shadow you drew?

Am I just a ghost you never knew?
Am I only a dream in your mind?
Why were you so unkind?
If I am only a nightmare of your sleepless night,
I am lost in your world of terror and fright.
Am I just a shadow you drew?

Lost Dreams

I wish I could close my eyes and forget all the problems of life, the
troubles that burn in my mind the sorrows, and the regrets gathered
like flowers in the fields of life lived well, were there a balm of forget-
fulness, I would consume it were it not death.
The flowers of hope and dreams grow in life's soils,
as I go through life's hardships and toils,
I wish I could close my eyes and forget all the problems of life, the
troubles that burn in my mind the sorrows, and the regrets gathered
like flowers in the fields of life lived well, were there a balm of forget-
fulness, I would consume it were it not death.
I gather troubles like forget-me-nots and daisy chains,
they are life pains and banes,
I wish I could close my eyes and forget all the problems of life, the
troubles that burn in my mind the sorrows, and the regrets gathered
like flowers in the fields of life lived well, were there a balm of forget-
fulness, I would consume it were it not death.
The flowers of hope and dreams grow in life's soils,
as I go through life's hardships and toils,

My hopes and cares would no longer there, they would fly away like
butterflies in the air,
Taking away my worries and cares
But it's like catching a snowflake, when you do, it's no longer there.

I wish I could close my eyes and forget all the problems of life
I wish I could close my eyes and forget all the problems of life,

THE MAGICIANS: OUR SOLEMN HOUR- SONG

Spoken

Oh My God, what is that monster doing to that corpse?

It's coming back to life!

Chorus

I can't believe it,

I don't believe what I just saw!

I saw a dead man come back to life,

I know that man!

He can't be dead!

Verse

I saw him return to life but how?

What was that monster doing?

Was he the dead man somehow?

Chorus

I can't believe it,

I don't believe what I just saw!

I saw a dead man come back to life,

I know that man!

He can't be dead!

Verse

What can I do?

Who can I tell?

Will he come after me?

Chorus

I can't believe it,

I don't believe what I just saw!

I saw a dead man come back to life,

I know that man!

He can't be dead!

Coda

I can't believe it,

I don't believe what I just saw!

I saw a dead man come back to life,

I know that man!

He can't be dead!

Spoken

Dr Death came back to life

will he come for me?

RACHEL LAWSON

THE GOTHIC POETS DEPARTMENT A SONG

Spoken

Welcome to The Gothic Poets Department,

Chorus

Welcome to The Gothic Poets Department, before you depart,

Home of the dark side of the art,

We all bear a dark heart,

Verse

Our founder of the league was Poe,

If we go to dark for you let us know,

we'll let you go,

Chorus

Welcome to The Gothic Poets Department, before you depart,

Home of the dark side of the art,

We all bear a dark heart,

Verse

We like the darkness of the night,

It really is a good sight,

though it causes in some great fright,

Chorus

Welcome to The Gothic Poets Department, before you depart,

Home of the dark side of the art,

We all bear a dark heart,

I know our art can scare some,

don't be glum,

not all to our art do succumb,

Chorus

Welcome to The Gothic Poets Department, before you depart,

Home of the dark side of the art,

We all bear a dark heart,

Chorus

Welcome to The Gothic Poets Department, before you depart,

We all bear a dark heart

Coda

Welcome to The Gothic Poets Department, before you depart,

We all bear a dark heart

Welcome to The Gothic Poets Department, before you depart,

Welcome to The Gothic Poets Department, before you depart,

(we part)

(we part)

ABOUT THE AUTHOR

Rachel is a lover of gothic

poetry and the stories of Emily Dickinson, Poe, and other poets and

writers. She writes in a gothic sometimes romantic, and somewhat eclectic style

Is a classic, prolific writer.

Contact Rachel via her website

Where she writes

https://allpoetry.com/The_Poette

Good Reads Page

https://www.goodreads.com/author/show/17771936.Rachel_La
wson

Website

http://www.rachellawsonpoet.yolasite.com/

YouTube songs are sung here

https://www.youtube.com/@BlakeAlexander-kq8qq

Spotify Artist Profile

https://open.spotify.com/artist/1G9bsRFWnpq2RgNcrJ7Jmw?s
i=SvwykHkxQtGarCJM6Ijefw

Rachel Lawson, YouTube Topic

https://www.youtube.com/channel/UC2L3-DWz4IupjemyvNvf
rwA

Song Death Called to Me on YouTube

https://youtu.be/y9UcyVqiXjs

www.ingramcontent.com/pod-product-compliance
Lightning Source LLC
Chambersburg PA
CBHW052225150726
48002CB00003B/1277